COVENTRY TRANSPORT
1940-1974

COVENTRY TRANSPORT
1940-1974

ROGER BAILEY

First published in 2007

Reprinted in 2013 by
The History Press
The Mill, Brimscombe Port,
Stroud, Gloucestershire, GL5 2QG
www.thehistorypress.co.uk

© Roger Bailey, 2013

The right of Roger Bailey to be identified as the Author
of this work has been asserted in accordance with the
Copyrights, Designs and Patents Act 1988.

All rights reserved. No part of this book may be reprinted
or reproduced or utilised in any form or by any electronic,
mechanical or other means, now known or hereafter invented,
including photocopying and recording, or in any information
storage or retrieval system, without the permission in writing
from the Publishers.

British Library Cataloguing in Publication Data.
A catalogue record for this book is available from the British Library.

ISBN 978 0 7524 4237 2

Typesetting and origination by
The History Press
Printed in Great Britain

CONTENTS

	Acknowledgements	6
	Introduction	7
one	The Wartime Buses	9
two	Post-war Period	29
three	The Next Generation	81
four	Demonstrators and Coventry Buses after Service	123
five	Other Operators	139

ACKNOWLEDGEMENTS

Over the years there have been many people who have helped me, sometimes without even realising it. Special thanks go to David McGrory, a true Coventry historian; Mike Lane for the use of his photographs and Barry Greener a local transport enthusiast. Also, TN Lens for the use of many of the late A.J. Owen's photographs, who very generously made their views available and who provide a great service to the bus enthusiast.

Thanks also to fellow bus enthusiasts like David Wyles, Timothy Boads and Graham Bailey for their help in making this possible. A number of original photographs have been used where the original photography is not known: the author would welcome further information on the origins of these photographs. Thanks are also due to Arnold Chave, who proof read this edition and made helpful suggestions.

I would like to dedicate this book to the crews who worked on the buses over the many years that the city owned its own transport fleet. Especially my Mum and Dad, Maurine and Jim Bailey, who both worked on the buses in Coventry from the 1950s to the 1980s.

INTRODUCTION

This is the second book covering the history of transport in Coventry, starting in 1940 and finishing in 1974. For many readers most of this is within living memory and so it will be very easy to relate to many of the photographs and artefacts featured within these pages. So much has been lost already, but, hopefully, a little has been captured of an era long gone within these few pages.

By 1940 the city of Coventry was becoming a very different place, so much of it being devoted to war production, and so it was only a matter of time before any serious bombing took place over the city. The air raid that people remember the most took place on the night of 14 November 1940. The raid lasted eleven hours and saw 500 tons of high explosives and 30,000 fire bombs dropped. By the morning, besides all the destruction that had taken place, including the burning of the then current Coventry Cathedral, the tram system had been destroyed, never to be operated again. Surprisingly, the trams survived, a number being isolated around the city.

This and many other pressures led to a need for additional buses and over 100 vehicles, built to a utility design, were delivered during the war period. A good number were built on locally manufactured Daimler chassis, but there were also a number of Guys, a Bristol and even Bedford delivered. For the short term, hired buses helped fill the gap until new vehicles could be delivered. Normal services and those feeding into the various factories managed to keep going. But, by the end of the Second World War, it was a very tired fleet.

As soon as the opportunity arose, orders were placed for new buses. But as every other operator was doing the same and as many manufacturers were still trying to switch over from war production to peacetime manufacturing, it would take time for new buses to be delivered.

The first buses to arrive were produced by local companies, the Daimler chassis with Birmingham-based Metro-Cammell bodies for sixty people. Carrying on a tradition started in the 1930s, many of the early deliveries also had AEC engines. From 1948 and for the three following years 100 new buses arrived, all to the same specification. By the early 1950s, new deliveries were arriving, including a batch of unique Maudslay double-deckers, new single-deck buses and some interestingly odd choices like a Crossley and London-style type AEC RT, plus a couple of late deliveries with Daimler and not AEC engines. At the same time, many of the wartime deliveries were starting to be sent away for refurbishment and, in some cases, new bodies. Pre-war buses were now being withdrawn, to be followed by wartime buses, which had received little attention or were considered non-standard.

New deliveries continued and included the last built to a width of 7ft 6in, but with a new style of concealed front. Again they were fitted with Metro-Cammell bodies with, in this case, seats for fifty-eight passengers. By 1955 the first delivery of buses built to a width of 8ft arrived and for the first time, they were powered by Gardner engines. Until 1963 deliveries were of the same type, only the front engine cover changing along the way, with most having seats for sixty people, the later arrivals seeing an increase to sixty-three seats. To keep its hire fleet up-to-date, new coaches were delivered in 1959 and further vehicles followed in 1963.

But the tide was turning and when General Manager Ronald Fearnley retired in 1963, new ideas were introduced that saw the delivery of the first front-entrance rear-engined buses, in this case being based on the Leyland Atlantean with Willowbrook bodies. Repeat orders were placed for vehicles built by local company Daimler and they were delivered with a variety of body styles over the following years.

By 1965 one-man operation started to take hold and vehicles were ordered taking this into consideration. Initially single-decker orders – and later the double-decker orders too – were of vehicles for such use, with previously delivered vehicles eventually being converted. A variety of chassis were ordered, including Daimler but also Bedford, Commer (for welfare usage), Bristol and Ford. Very different when compared to the days of pure standardisation.

The year 1971 saw decimalisation, resulting in all the platform staff trained to deal with it, so that correct fares were paid on the day and, more importantly, the correct change given.

In 1974 ownership was transferred from Coventry City Council to the West Midlands Passenger Transport Executive and so an era came to an end. Hopefully this book and the previously published *Coventry Transport 1884–1940*, will capture a little of that history. To appeal to a wider audience, what follows is not a fleet list of vehicles operated, but more of a social history of what was a very important part of this historic city. This is also a personal journey which I hope you, the reader, will enjoy.

ONE
THE WARTIME BUSES

Not featured in *Coventry Transport 1884–1940* were buses bought second-hand from 1938 onwards for service in the city. They were a small mixture of four single-deck Leylands and four double-deck AECs, but all had been withdrawn by 1948. Here is one of the AECs from Halifax, with a camelback Hoyel open-stairs body numbered 4 (CP 8010). (Travel Lens)

Another from the batch of four ex-Halifax double-deck buses is number 5, re-bodied in 1942 by Brush. A further photograph, later in the chapter, shows a bus from the same batch with its original body. (Travel Lens)

Many buses were hired to cover for the loss of the tram system during the raid of the 14 November 1940 and the need for more buses. They came from London as well as many other places around the country. This photograph shows a number of them parked near the football ground as part of a dispersal system, to avoid losing vehicles during the bombing. They include buses from London, Halifax and Great Yarmouth.

One of the vehicles hired from London, seen here opposite Holy Trinity Church. This was ST 481 (GK 5312), an AEC Regent with LGOC body. (Travel Lens)

Part of an order for ten vehicles, only three actually arrived for service in the city. The others went to Midland Red and Hull. These were numbered 259–261 and were AEC Regents with Brush bodies delivered in 1942. Here they are seen with masked headlights with a National Westminster bank in the background.

Another from the same batch, but post-Second World War. The location is the original Pool Meadow. All three were withdrawn from service in 1958.

Bus number 284 was the solitary Bristol K5G with a body by Strachan delivered in 1942, being the first of over 100 buses built to the Ministry of Supply specifications with seats for fifty-six passengers. This post-war shot of the bus, after rebuilding by Nudd Brothers & Lockyer, was taken in the old Pool Meadow, with the bus on possible driver-training duty. Note the old city gate in the background.

A batch of single-deck buses were delivered the same year, being based on the Bedford OB and came with Roe utility bodies. The batch were numbered 290–298, this being possibly the only good surviving photograph of them. (Haynes)

Above: An aerial shot of what was later to become Broadgate. Note the devastation caused by war damage. In the middle there is both a single-deck Bedford and one of the four AEC Regents bought second-hand. The latter is probably bus number 7, which had been reconditioned in 1943. It is believed the photograph was taken between 1945 and 1947.

Opposite above: Other buses delivered for service in 1942 included a number based on the Guy chassis, the first being a batch numbered 285–289, and they came with bodies by Brush. The photograph was taken close to the old Smithfield, opposite Coventry Theatre, before the vehicle was rebuilt.

In rebuilt form, bus number 288 on a service extra, waiting on waste ground to the side of Pool Meadow and with Trinity Street in the far background.

Further buses based on the Guy chassis were delivered to Coventry the same year, this being number 300 with a body by Massey. Many of the Guys were underpowered and were slow and sluggish, hence why they spent so much time on service extras. It was withdrawn in 1959.

Further Guys – but fitted with bodies by Weymann – originally intended for Manchester Corporation, were numbered 302-309 when delivered and to Coventry in 1943. The batch are represented here by number 303, in its wartime grey livery with masked headlights. A National Westminster bank features in the background.

Another from the same batch, number 304, seen in Trinity Street with Holy Trinity Church to the right and Timothy White's chemist behind.

The next batch of buses were again Guys, numbered 310–315 and came with Park Royal bodies. Bus 315 is seen in the background in its wartime grey livery while a pre-war bus, number 237, is in front. Holy Trinity Church is in the background.

Bus number 316, seen here in Trinity Street, was part of a batch numbered 316–320. They were Daimler CWG5s with a Gardner engine, with bodies by Duple and delivered in 1943.

A nostalgic view in Pool Meadow showing bus 321 which, along with number 322, carried Massey bodywork and were both based on the Daimler CWG5 chassis. Seen behind is a single-deck Daimler waiting to go to Berkswell on the 19 route. Notice the bus queues.

Sister vehicle 322, about to pull out of Harnall Lane bus garage ready to go into service at peaktime. It looks like summer with the light-coloured uniform worn by the conductress. To the right are the offices used by the crews to pay in their money after their shift.

Bus 324 is a Guy Arab with Weymann bodywork, part of a batch numbered 323–329. Seen here on the waste ground to the side of Pool Meadow, with the bus shelters in the background.

Shown here is a low-height bus, number 330, a Guy Arab with a Brush body that was exchanged with Middlesbrough Corporation for a Leyland originally allocated to Coventry.

An interesting shot of bus 332, a Guy Arab II with Park Royal body and part of the batch 331–335. This was rebuilt by the bodybuilder Bond in the early 1950s, to a more relaxed style and was one of a number so treated. The photograph is believed to have been taken outside the Bond's works located in the Manchester area. The bus had been re-seated to sixty-seat capacity in 1949. (Bond)

At long last, the combination that Coventry bought many of before war broke out: a Daimler chassis with an AEC engine but to a wartime specification, the CWA6. Bus 337 – the batch being numbered 336–338 – had Duple bodywork, delivered in 1944. Virtually all the remaining deliveries during the war were to the same specification. Photographed in Corporation Street with the new Co-op being built in the background.

Another similar bus 340 (EKV 940), this time with a body by NCME and part of a batch numbered 339–341. Seen here in later life in Pool Meadow Bus Station.

The last of the wartime buses to remain in service was number 344 (EKV 344), seen here at the Devonshire Arms terminus of service 9A on its last day in service. Originally part of the batch 342–345, which were again Daimlers with bodywork by Weymann and later rebuilt by Bond. (Greener)

Another view of the same bus on its last day in service in August 1964. In its time with Coventry it had covered about 500,000 miles in twenty years of service. (Greener)

Bus 346 (EKV 946) was delivered in 1943. A Guy Arab with Park Royal body and seen here in post-war Broadgate, when the statue of Lady Godiva (just out of shot) was located in the middle of an island.

Bus 348 (EKV 948), part of the 347–356 batch which were Daimler CWA6s with NCME bodywork delivered in 1944. This photograph was taken at the back of Harnall Lane bus garage. (Greener)

From the same batch is bus 353, standing in Broadgate with Broadgate House and the new shops nearing completion.

Another bus from the same batch, but this time in the original Pool Meadow Bus Station, with bus 356 waiting for passengers. Note the one-　　man air-raid shelter on the right and in the background under the canopy, the kiosk which was run by a blind man.

The last Guy Arabs delivered were batch 357–360, with bodies by Strachan that resembled the Park Royal utility, in 1945. This is bus 357 (EKV 957).

The last four batches delivered were all based on the Daimler CWA6, in this case numbered 361–362 with Brush bodies. This shows bus 361 (EKV961) on its delivery and, looking carefully, you can see the slatted seats inside, something that was not very popular with passengers.

Bus 363 seen here in it later guise as the Coventry Carol Bus, was part of a batch numbered 363–372, all with Duple bodies delivered in 1944. The bus would travel around the city at night, usually with children from local schools aboard, collecting money for the Lord Mayor's charity appeal. Here it is seen parked outside the old fire station.

Another from the same batch, but this time in normal service, here seen in Pool Meadow Bus Station, with the old fire station in the background.

Bus 376 (FDU 376), part of the 373–376 batch delivered in 1945 with Duple bodywork, seen here at the back of Harnall Lane bus garage.

The last delivery of wartime specification buses, but to a more relaxed style, were the batch 377–386, again with Duple bodies, mostly delivered in 1945, with the last two entering service in 1946. This is bus 380 (FDU 380) after rebuilding by Bond, seen in Spon End under the railway bridge.

A line-up of buses, including a number of wartime buses, in Harnall Lane garage, being washed for service the following day. (Travel Lens)

A postcard of a 'blitzed' Broadgate, showing Hereford Street in the background, probably taken before 1947.

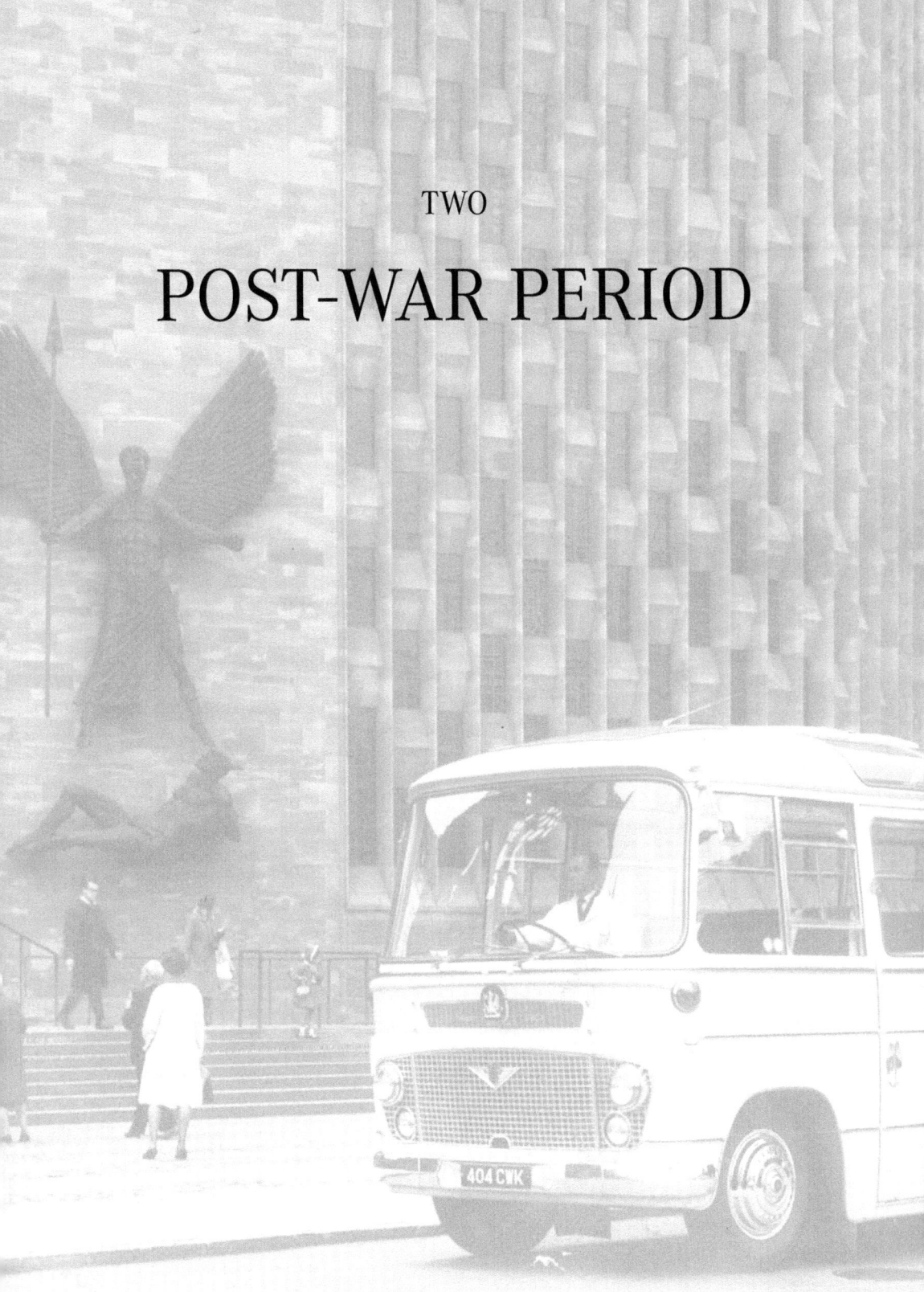

TWO
POST-WAR PERIOD

Orders were placed for new buses but due to demand from all operators, it took a while before the first new arrivals appeared. Deliveries commenced in 1948, the first ninety-five being Daimler CVA6s with sixty-seat Metro-Cammell bodies. The last bus arrived two years later. This is bus 16 (FHP 16), on its way to the fairground after departure from Pool Meadow Bus Station.

A good photograph of bus 19 (FHP 19), renumbered 419 in 1966 so as to avoid duplication with the arrival of Daimler Fleetline 19. It was withdrawn the same year and is seen at the top of Trinity Street with Owen Owen's in the background.

Bus number 55 (GKV 55) in Broadgate, not long before it was withdrawn in 1966, with the more modern fleet names along the sides and a painted radiator similar to bus number 4, which was normally chrome. It later served the city as a training bus, one of the first of many used to train drivers to work for Coventry Transport. Seven from this batch served this purpose. (Greener)

Bus 58 (GKV 58) waiting near the entrance to Pool Meadow Bus Station on a summer's day, with a more modern Daimler CVG6 in the background. (Travel Lens – G Lamb)

Bus 60 (GKV 60) waiting to run on a special service for football fans. These buses, and some that followed, had a single rear-destination blind. The rear-destination blind on Sandy Lane buses showed a destination, but Harnall Lane buses showed a route number.

Opposite above: Bus 77 (GKV 77) on a duplicate service passing the Coventry Theatre during the 1960s. The bus was withdrawn in 1964. Note the D. Di ice cream van to the right, a company once famous in the city.

Opposite below: In delivered condition, bus 90 (GKV 90) as seen in 1950, taken by the manufacturer before entering service. It lasted sixteen years.

SERVICE EXTRA
CITY
POOL MEADOW
GKV 77
THE COVENTRY THEATRE

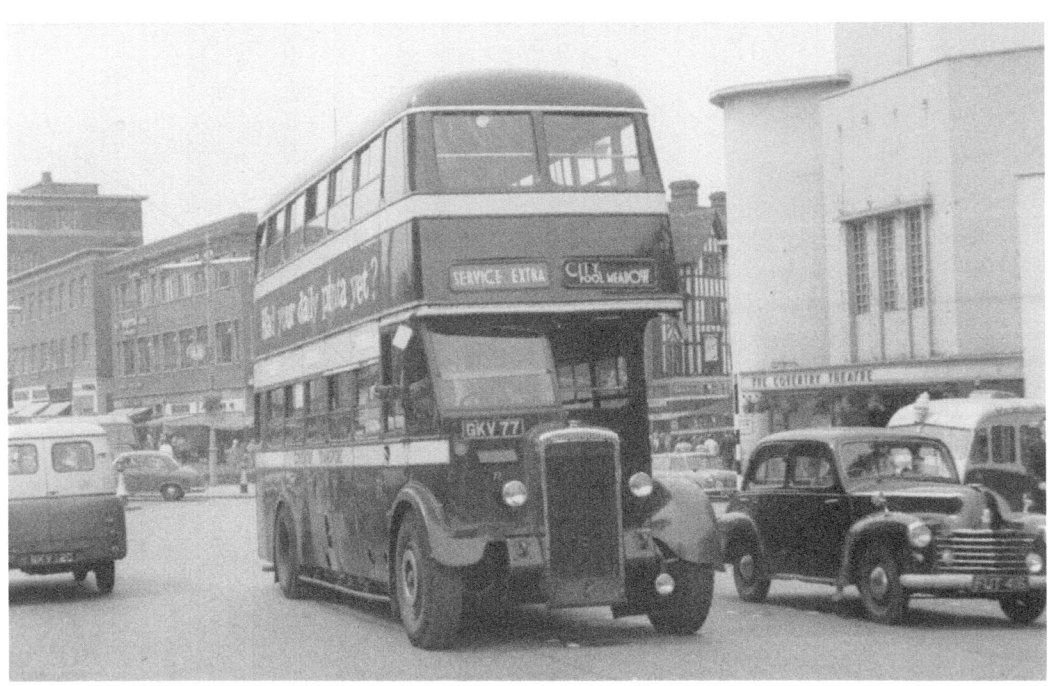

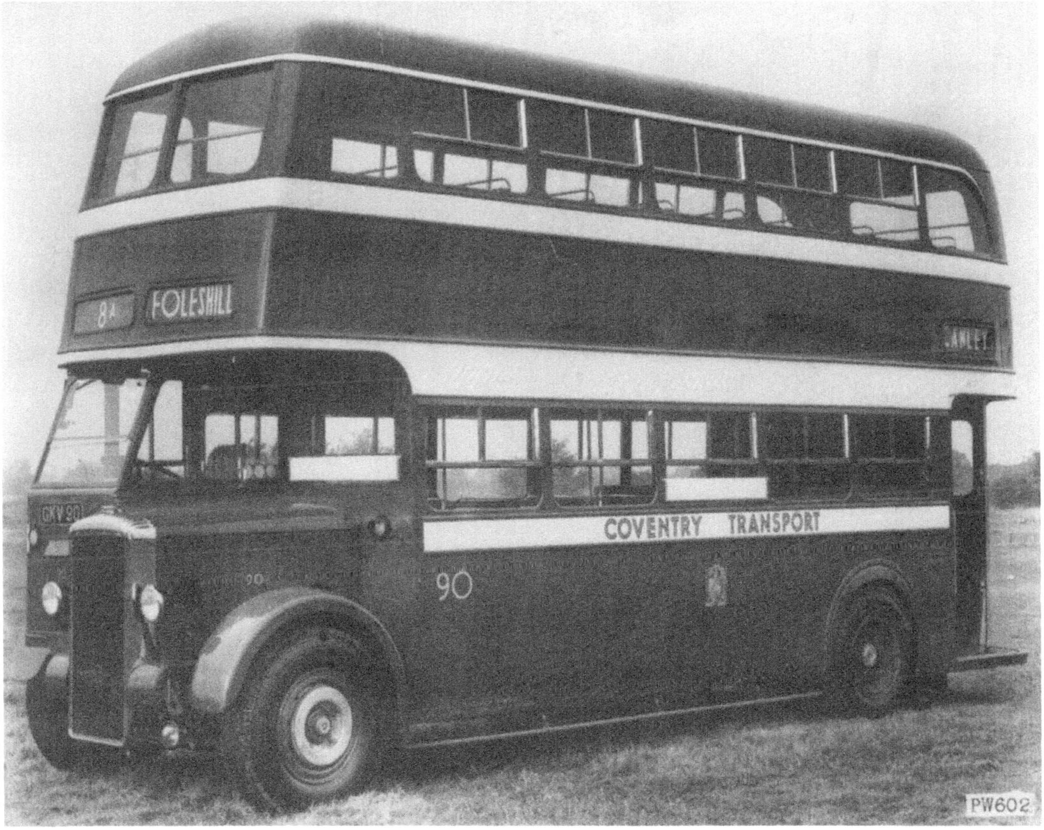
8A
FOLESHILL
GKV 90
COVENTRY TRANSPORT
90
PW602

A fleet of sixteen single-deck buses, based on the Daimler CVD6 chassis, arrived in 1949, replacing mostly pre-war vehicles. Bodies were by Brush and seating was for thirty-four passengers. This photograph shows delivery of the first, number 101 (GKV 101), next to a bus it was replacing. The location is the front of Harnall Lane garage.

The same bus after entering service, about to run on the Outer Circle Tour seen here in Wheatley Street near the old mill. Amongst other things, on view on this tour was the new housing estate at Canley!

Above: Bus 112 (HKV 112), photographed in what was probably the most typical shot of these vehicles, waiting its turn on the 19 route, near the entrance to Pool Meadow Bus Station. A number of these vehicles were often used on a special service for the AWA Works, mostly based at Baginton, to shuttle people to the company's Lutterworth site.

Right: Bus 113 at Harnall Lane garage, and two others numbered 111 & 114 had been converted to dual purpose with thirty coach seats in 1954. Note the metal stripes along the sides which all three carried after the conversion.

Another of the three conversions, this time bus 114, as seen in Pool Meadow in 1965, waiting to go on the 19 Berkswell service. It was withdrawn from service two years later. The dog's name is Duke! (Lane)

An interior photograph of one of the three buses converted for coach use, looking towards the front of the vehicle and clearly showing the upgraded seating.

The last of the batch, number 116, after arriving from operating service 19, the main service route for these vehicles. It is parked up in front of the inspector's kiosk in Pool Meadow Bus Station. (Greener)

Delivered in 1951, one of two Daimlers, number 97/98 (GKV 97/98) with Daimler engines and fluorescent lighting inside. Number 98 waits near the inspector's box in Pool Meadow Bus Station.

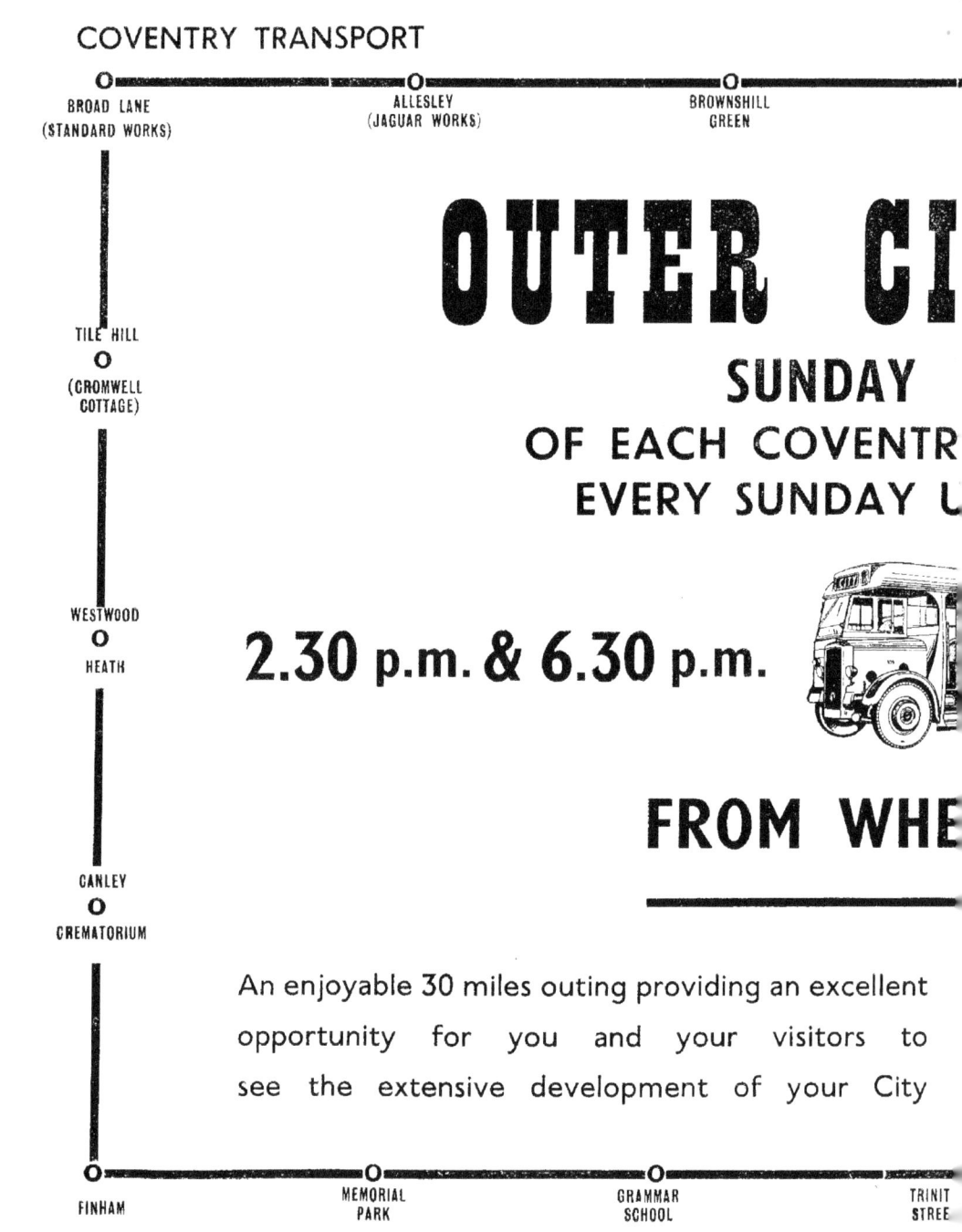

One of a series of adverts which promoted local events and issues. In this case the Outer Circle Tour using the newly delivered single-deck buses is advertised. There were two tours a day. The bus featured is 105, which still exists today as it has been preserved.

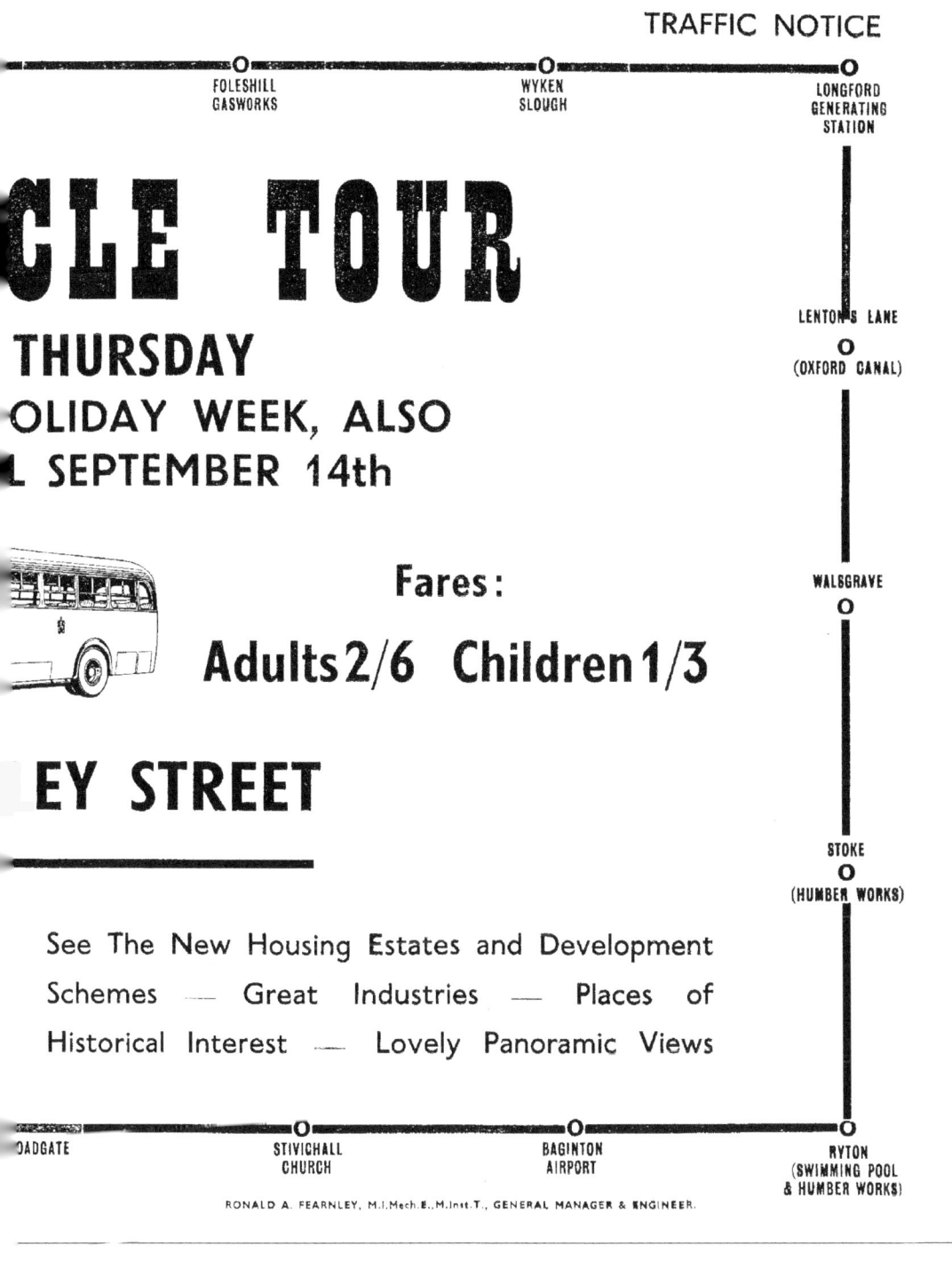

Another nostalgic poster, as displayed in the interior of many of the buses, located above the windows on each deck. In this case, Midget Car Racing at Brandon Speedway in 1951 is advertised. All adverts carried details of how to get there by bus – something not so relevant today perhaps.

R RACING
NDON

BUSES LEAVE WHEATLEY STREET
FROM 1.30 P.M.
RETURNING AFTER EACH MEETING

Fare 6d. Single
NO RETURN TICKETS OR CHILDREN'S FARES

RONALD A. FEARNLEY, M.I.Mech.E., M.Inst.T.
GENERAL MANAGER & ENGINEER

A photograph taken from the top deck of a bus, looking into Sandy Lane garage around 1957, showing a variety of buses including one of the three AEC Regents number 261 on the right-hand side. (Bailey)

A postcard of Broadgate outside Owen Owen, taken in the late 1950s, showing both a post-war and wartime bus in service.

The unique number 99 (GKV 99), being an AEC Regent III with Metro-Cammell fifty-six-seat body. Identical in body style to those produced for service in London, except for the combination of this make of body fixed on an AEC chassis. After much delay it entered service in 1951 and lasted until 1964. This photograph was taken in Broadgate with the near completion of Broadgate House in the background.

The photograph of bus 99 is taken outside the main garage at Sandy Lane, where all odd numbered buses were based after the depot was opened. All even numbered buses were based at Harnall Lane. Drivers remember that what looked like a coat hanger behind the driver's seat, was actually the starter!

Interior shots are rare, but this shows number 99 again, this time from inside looking towards the platform. So many of the bus crews remember that the platform pole always gave you dirty black hands when you held it.

Another unusual bus was a Crossley, numbered 100 (GKV 100) and painted in a reverse livery, like bus 205 similarly treated when delivered in the 1930s. It had a Metro-Cammell body with fifty-eight seats and like 99, was delivered in 1951. It is seen here when being used on the Inner Circle route.

Another photograph of the same bus, this time parked up in Pool Meadow. This vehicle saw mechanical changes throughout its life, including different gearboxes, starting service with a crashbox.

Seen here in early 1960s Broadgate on a service extra, bus 100 is flanked by others in the fleet including one of the single-deckers.

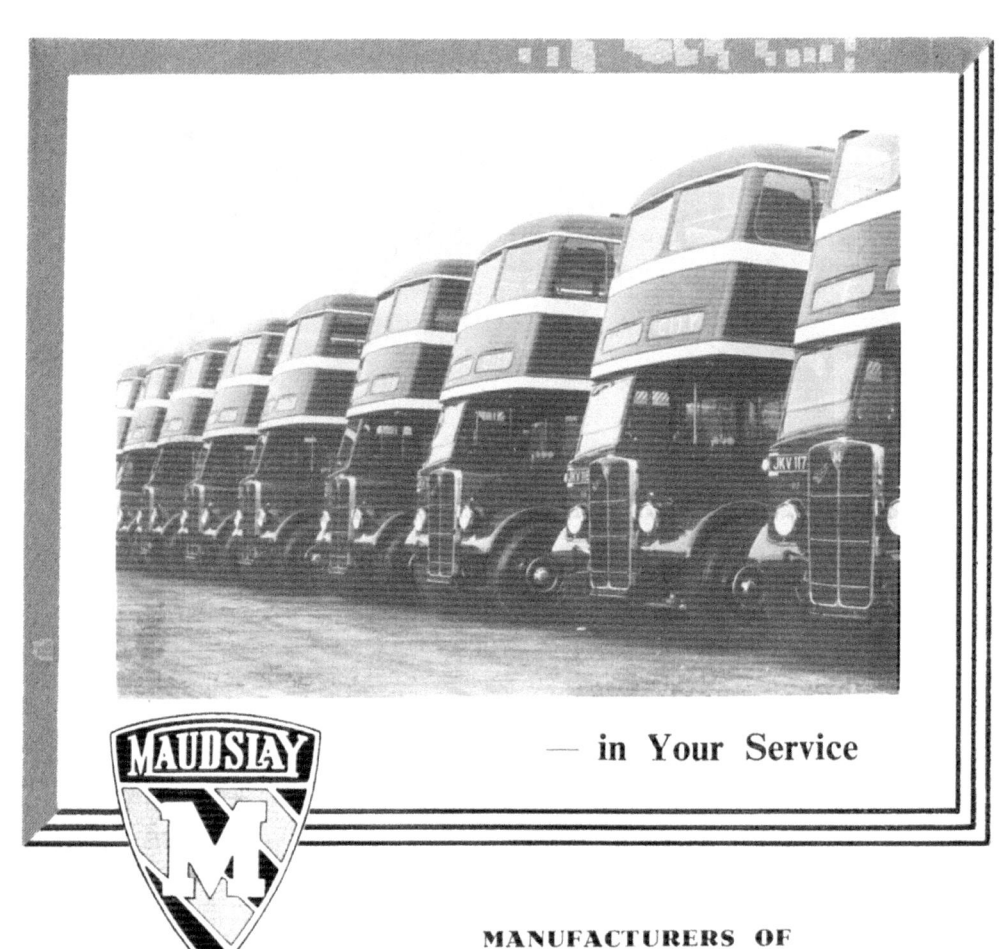

A copy of an advert featuring the fleet of unique Maudslay Regents which entered service in Coventry during 1951. Later in life these buses were used on service extras or works specials. One such service being the number 15a that linked the AWA Works at Baginton with the Jaguar car plant. The service would take workers home from one and deliver them to work at the other.

An unusual photograph of one of this batch of nine vehicles, with bus 117 (JKV 117) being tested on a tilt machine when new. They all had Metro-Cammell bodies, but of a different style to those on other vehicles in service in the city.

Bus 119 parked up in Pool Meadow, a popular location for taking pictures of buses. These vehicles were basically AEC Regents, but were assembled at the Maudslay factory at the same time as other vehicles, mostly fire engines. They were the only post-war Maudslay double-deck buses.

A shot of the front of Harnall Lane bus garage where two of the Maudslay buses are waiting to go out on service as service extras. The last of them were withdrawn from service in 1965.

Bus 124 in the yard at the back of Harnall Lane bus garage, where many of the fleet were parked overnight. (Travel Lens – G. Lamb)

A classic shot of one of these rare vehicles, in this case number 124. The last had been withdrawn by 1965.

The next batch of buses to arrive were the last examples built to a width of 7ft 6in and were the first with enclosed radiators, referred to as Birmingham-style fronts. Numbered 126–165, they were mostly delivered in 1952, again with Metro-Cammell bodies with seats for fifty-eight passengers. This is bus 131 (KVC 131) on Hearsall Lane in 1971, being withdrawn the same year. (Lane)

A rare interior shot of bus 140, looking towards the platform and taken before it entered service. It was withdrawn in 1971 after nineteen years service.

A number of buses parked-up awaiting service, including bus 143, withdrawn from service in 1971. In the background are the partly built swimming baths in Fairfax Street. When new, the front destination handles were under the upper-deck canopy, but were modified to a position above the radiator cap.

A line-up of four members of the batch, with a completed swimming baths in the background. Some of these buses would be waiting to go into service at peak time. Bus 151 was withdrawn in 1972 and bus 152 went in 1968, the latter spending some time as a driver-trainer vehicle, one of four from this batch.

Bus 144 parked up at Keresley Works in Watery Lane, in use until the expansion took place at Sandy Lane in 1966. Much work was carried out here including body repair and mechanical repairs, for example, and it was first brought into use in 1942.

The front cover of the 1954 timetable, with the first of the post-war buses featured on the front.

The following series of four photographs were all taken in September 1955, in three cases showing the huge bus queues waiting for buses to take them home. Such sights would be unbelievable in the twenty-first century. Note the queues in Pool Meadow Bus Station waiting for the bus to Tile Hill and other destinations, but not a bus in sight.

A second photograph in Pool Meadow, this time from the other end looking down past the bus stops towards where the Willenhall bus departs from.

A queue stretching from Trinity Street into Hales Street, waiting for the bus to Coundon, the bus stop being located near the Smithfield Hotel.

The fourth photograph shows a view looking up Trinity Street when it had two-way traffic and cars were allowed to park down the central reservation. Note bus 356, a wartime Daimler to the left, where Sainsbury's was later built.

Above: New buses were needed, so buses 166–215 (RWK 166–190, SKV 191–215) were delivered between late 1955 running into 1957. They were the first in the city built to a width of 8ft, with MCW Orion bodies and Birmingham fronts. They were also the first to be delivered in what became a city standard, Daimler CVG6 with Gardner engine and MCW body. In this case the buses came with seats for sixty passengers. This is bus 178 parked up at the back of Harnall Lane bus garage. (Bailey)

Left: Bus 179 later in life, after having just been painted into the new colour scheme of Marshall red and Shetland ivory, one of only two in the batch treated such. Here it is seen in Sandy Lane garage as an odd-numbered bus, but now also showing a garage plate, which never used to be carried. Sandy Lane was officially opened by the Lord Mayor on 1 September 1954. Replacing Folshill Road Depot, it was at this point bus allocations were split according to their number. Odd numbers went to Sandy Lane and even numbers to Harnall Lane. (Bailey)

Bus 184 seen parked up in the new Pool Meadow Bus Station, not long after it had been finished. Note in the background that the De Vere Hotel had yet to be built, but the car park for Sainsbury's had. (Bailey)

A line-up along the side of Sandy Lane bus garage led by bus 187, which was withdrawn from service in 1972. The batch were later fitted with flashes located beneath the lower-deck windows. Harnall Lane buses received a curved unit while Sandy Lane buses received a rectangular unit with silver edges. (Bailey)

An interior photograph of bus 189, taken before entering service. You can see along the sides and above the windows the space where the interior adverts used to be displayed – similar to those featured in this book. This bus, along with four others from the batch, became driver-training vehicles, introducing a yellow livery for such a task.

Bus 194 here seen in Broadgate passing a number of other fleet members. The photograph was taken in 1971, the year before it was withdrawn. (Lane)

Bus 213 parked in Pool Meadow Bus Station, with the student flats being built for what was then the Lanchester Polytechnic. (Bailey)

A postcard of the era, showing an impressive line-up of buses in Broadgate, with the famous Lady Godiva statue in its original position before it was later moved.

A rare rear view, in this case of bus 213 waiting in Sandy Lane bus garage just before going into service. The photograph was taken for C & L Sales, whose advert is seen on the rear of the vehicle.

Opposite above: The view is from the rear entrance to Harnall Lane bus garage, showing some of the early buses built to 8ft wide parked up. This photograph was taken in 1969. (Bailey).

Opposite below: An impressive display of the blinds used in all the buses at the time. Bus 175 is proudly showing itself off at the rear of Sandy Lane garage. (Travel Lens)

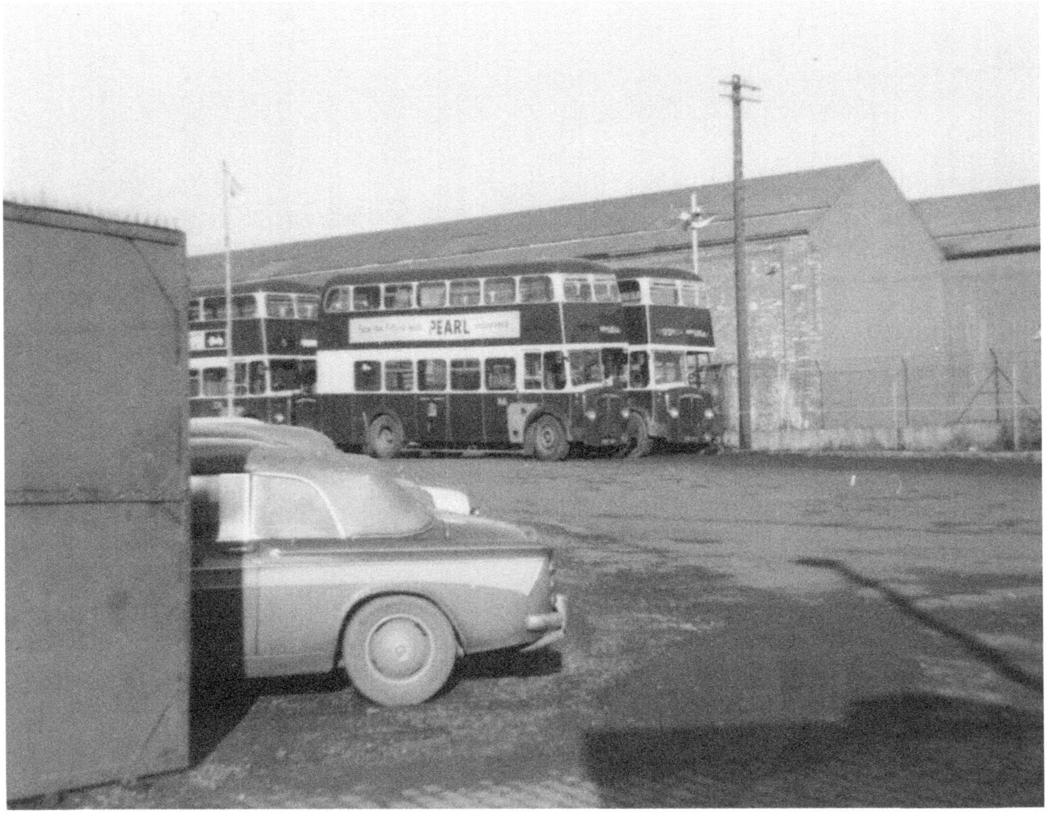
PEARL

SERVICE EXTRA
SCHOOL BUS
FOOTBALL SPECIAL
PRIVATE
STADIUM
CORLEY
A.C. WICKMAN
COURTHOUSE GREEN
PARKSIDE
JAGUAR BROWNS LANE
SERVICE EXTRA
SPEEDWAY
PRIVATE
HUMBER WORKS
WHITLEY
FLETCHAMSTEAD
HEARSALL COMMON
MEMORIAL PARK
STOKE HEATH
CHAPELFIELDS
CITY
CHEYLESMORE
RADFORD
HEN LANE
HOLBROOKS
LONDON ROAD
LYTHALL LANE

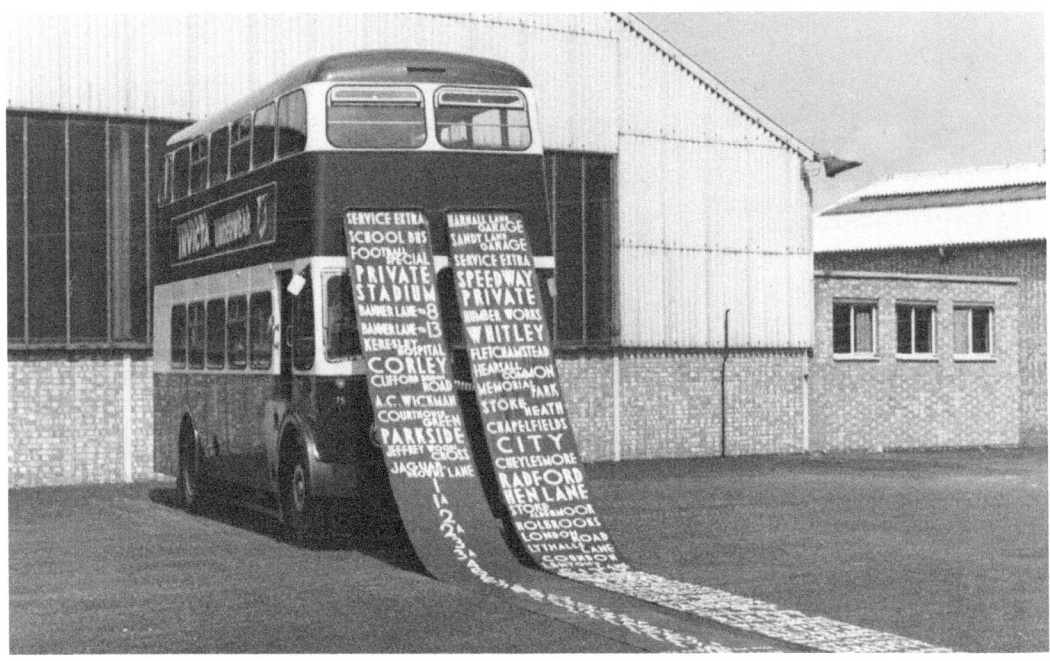

An advert for Owen Owen, then the key store in the city centre, as found in a bus timetable of the 1950s. Very much of its period, with even the bus crew running off to shop!

The front cover of the 1956 bus timetable, with one of the recently delivered buses on the front, giving it a more modern image.

Bus 215, a Daimler CVG6 with MCW body for sixty passengers, and the first to have the new front, being converted from having a Birmingham front to the later Manchester type. It carried a smaller scroll than others of this type. It is seen here painted in a later variant of the maroon and cream livery with the coat of arms above the destination screen. (Bailey)

A photograph taken in the early 1960s in the despatch area of Sandy Lane bus garage. In the photograph are John Flynn, Colman O'Donughue, Maurine Bailey and Roy Crosswell. Behind are the duty sheets for the bus crews. (Bailey)

Bus 216 (VWK 216), another Daimler CVG6 with the standard MCW body with seats for sixty people. It was part of the batch numbered 216–265 and delivered in 1958. Note its Harnall Lane plate above the driver's cab, a much later addition, plus the coat of arms above the side windows. There were many experiments with the fleet livery and position of the fleet name and coat of arms during the early 1970s. In the cab is Maurine Bailey, one of the first three women drivers for Coventry, not long after she had passed her test. (Bailey)

Bus 217, seen here in Pool Meadow in the third set of bus bays added many years after the bus station had been built. In the background is one of the three single-deck Daimler Freelines, resplendent in the sky blue colour scheme as used for coach operations. It is probably waiting for use on the 19 Berkswell route. The photograph was taken in 1966.

As delivered new, bus 221 outside the front of Sandy Lane bus garage. This was one of five which had an experimental livery change, the roof being all cream. Later on, another batch were delivered in a similar scheme for the opening of the new Coventry Cathedral.

Very much the standard of the fleet for many years, bus 235, a Daimler CVG6 seen at the top of Trinity Street coming into Broadgate during 1965. (Lane)

The first of two views of Broadgate, in this case taken from St Michael's Tower and showing the original position of the Lady Godiva statue and the buses waiting around the edge for their passengers.

Another photograph of the same scene, but taken from a different angle, in use as it was originally intended to be.

Maurine and Jim Bailey with their son Roger, taken in about 1960, dressed in their Coventry Transport uniforms. (Bailey)

Jim Bailey, this time on the back of bus 247, not long after he had started working in Coventry, having previously worked for Midland Red. (Bailey)

Three new coaches were added to the fleet in 1959: 401–403 (XRW 401-403) being Daimler Freelines with Willowbrook Viking bodies for forty-one passengers. The first, when new, is seen here posing for a photograph in Warwick Castle. (Bailey)

Later on, when all three had been converted for use as buses, mainly for the 19 bus route, they had full blinds fitted as well as ticket machines. Here are two of them waiting in Pool Meadow.

The last of the three coaches is seen here turning into Corporation Street in its short-lived sky blue coach livery. All had been withdrawn by 1970. They were never fast, keeping to a speed of 40mph. (Greener)

A new batch of buses arrived in 1959, numbered 266–290, again to the standard Daimler/MCW combination for double-deckers. This is number 271 (XVC 271) coming round Broadgate. You can clearly see the temporary shops in the background, which included a Lyon's tearoom. Bus 281 when delivered, was fitted with a Daimler engine and not the usual Gardner.

The next batch of arrivals numbered 291–312 arrived in 1961, this time being fitted with seats for sixty-three passengers. They had cream roofs and were known as the festival buses, linking in with the opening of Coventry Cathedral. This example is bus 293 (293 RW), coming out of Pool Meadow with the Midland Red offices on the left. It is worth noting that as of March this year, there were 333 buses in the fleet, of which forty were wartime survivors. (Lane)

The last batch of old-style buses delivered were numbered 313–337 in 1963, bus 318 (318 CRW) is seen here passing the fire station, which has now become a restaurant and bar.

Bus 330 in the later livery of Marshall red and Shetland ivory. Seen here in Broadgate with Holy Trinity Church in the background. (Travel Lens – G. Lumb)

Bus 332 in Pool Meadow, showing an experimental livery in maroon and cream, but with the coat of arms above the side windows. One suggestion for this was to save on costs of replacing this, if the bus was in a collision. (Travel Lens)

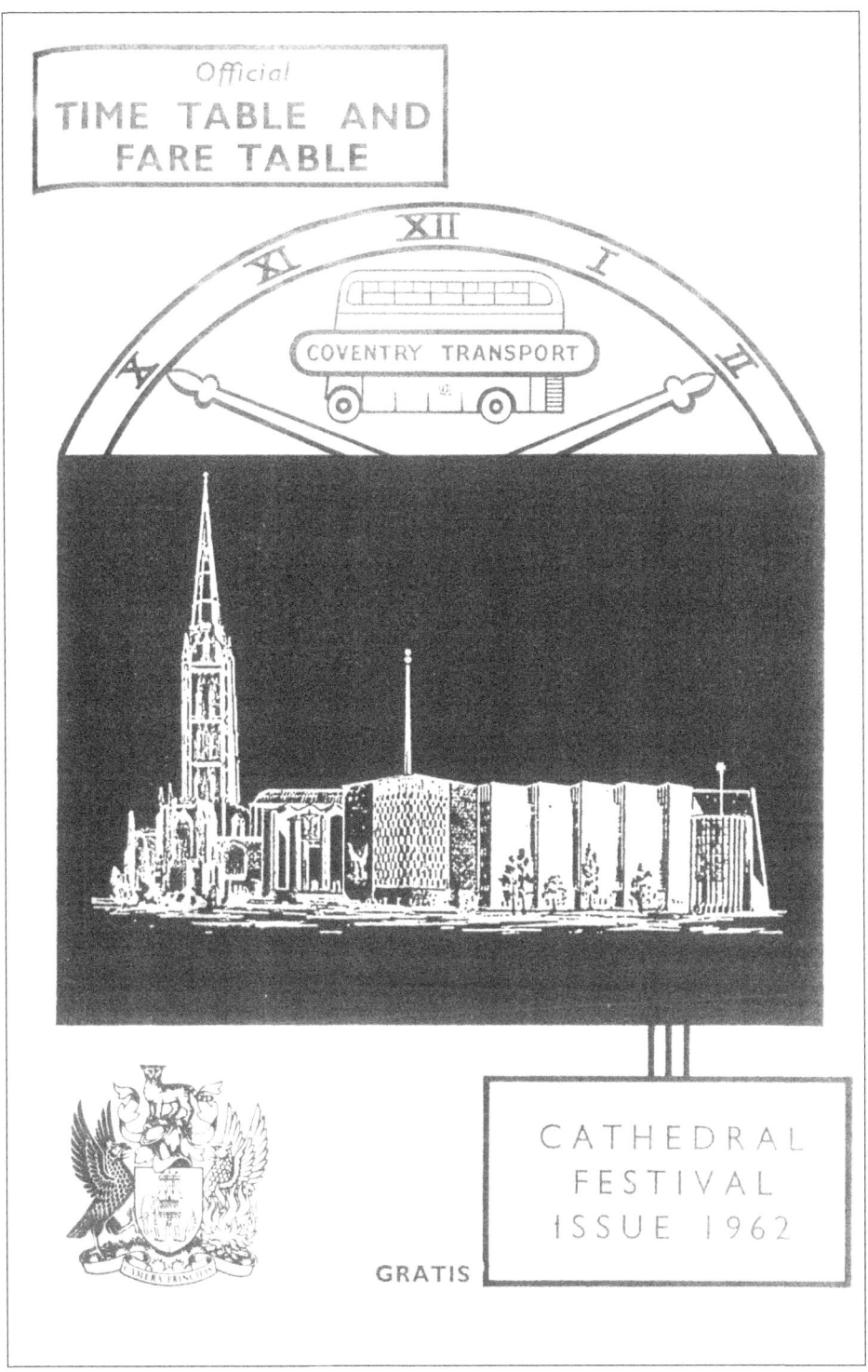

To celebrate the opening of the new Coventry Cathedral, the bus timetable for 1962 featured an image of the building on the front.

Three new coaches were delivered in 1964, 404–406 (404 CWK, CDU 405/406B) being Bedfords with forty-one-seat Duple bodies. This is an official photograph of the first, number 404, outside Coventry Cathedral.

Two Coventry bus inspectors, Tom Paddy and Ron Batter, standing in front of coach 404 in Sandy Lane bus garage forecourt.

The second of the batch, number 405, is seen here in Sandy Lane bus garage showing a rare rear view. You can clearly see the body style and the use of the livery. (Bailey)

Coach 406 seen while on an excursion. Coventry Corporation was one of a very few corporations that had a licence to run coach trips outside its city boundary. (Travel Lens – G. Lamb)

Coach 406 seen approaching Hearsall on a private hire. Note the white coat worn by the driver.

An interior photograph of one of the coaches, looking down towards the driver. Only a few of the bus drivers were given the opportunity to drive the coaches. (Bailey)

A fourth coach delivered at the time was this Ford with a twenty-five-seat Martin Walker body. It is seen here outside Harnall Lane garage with one of the single-deck Bedford buses in the background.

Another shot of the same vehicle was on driver-learner duties, seen here in Pool Meadow. In the background, they have still to build the De Vere Hotel.

This is a poster for the 1964 Coventry Horse Show that used to be held in the War Memorial Park.

SHOW

**FIRST EVENT
10.00 a.m.**

AT

ARK

NCE)

VILLAGE
DGATE

**FOXHUNTER
COMPETITION**

★

SHOW PONIES

★

**OPEN JUMPING
COMPETITION**

★

**INTER-CLUB RELAY
COMPETITION**

★

GYMKHANA

★

"LONG JOHN WHISKY"
OPEN JUMPING COMPETITION

N. McDONALD, M.Inst.T.,
GENERAL MANA

The front cover of a brochure used to promote the use of coaches owned by Coventry Transport.

THREE

THE NEXT GENERATION

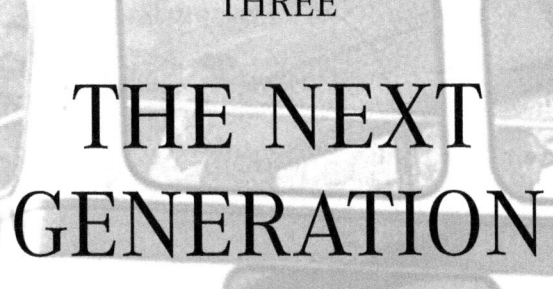

A rare shot of the very first delivery of the batch 338–359, Leyland Atlanteans with bodywork by Willowbrook and seventy-six seats. While number 338 was being shown at the Commercial Motorshow in London, bus 340 (CDU 338B) had arrived at Harnall Lane bus garage in September 1964 and is seen parked up with bus 98, which was withdrawn within weeks. Note the new-style livery used on all subsequent deliveries. (Bailey)

The first of many: bus 338 is seen here in service in Pool Meadow, with its original new-style colour scheme. They were ordered originally because they were cheaper, but there was much protest concerning the order not going to the local company, Daimler. The batch were stored at the Keresley Works until a dispute about their use could be sorted out with the union and crews, finally entering service in early 1965. (Bailey)

Bus 342 waiting at Sandy Lane bus garage, even though it is an even-numbered bus with a Harnall Lane bus garage code. In actual fact, it was waiting to go back to its garage after being used on a Sandy Lane bus route. (Bailey)

Bus 345 waiting to depart from Pool Meadow, going to the Armstrong Whitworth Works at Baginton, when aeroplanes were still being made there. When they first went into service they were fitted with green bulbs to illuminate the destination blinds, which was soon changed to white bulbs as it had proved difficult to read.

One of the Leyland Atlanteans, bus 347 is parked up in Pool Meadow. Note the construction of student accommodation being built for what was then the Lanchester Polytechnic. The front display could not be viewed from the cab, so the conductor had to stand outside to tell the driver which display to stop on.

Bus 349 departing from Pool Meadow with the Midland Red offices and famous clock tower in the background, taken in 1971. The rear destination had to be changed from the outside using handles from the rear upper-deck canopy, reached by a step on the rear bustle. (Lane)

The cover of the 1965 Coventry Transport timetable has an image of the latest additions to the fleet, one of the Leyland Atlanteans.

Waiting to depart for Willenhall is number 350, shown in its new livery of Marshall red and Shetland ivory. (Travel Lens – G. Lamb)

The next batch of new vehicles reverted back to the local manufacturer, Daimler. These were Daimler Fleetlines, again Willowbrook-bodied buses for seventy-six passengers. The fleet numbers were 360– 381 and this is bus 361 (CRW 361C). (Greener)

Bus 366 in Pool Meadow with Marshall red and Shetland ivory livery. Its body was identical to the previous batch, but had an additional opening window on the upper deck. (Bailey)

Parked up in Sandy Lane bus garage is bus 377, painted in one of the experimental versions of the original livery, with the coat of arms behind the drivers cab and a modern version of the fleet name. Six were converted in 1969, the others following in 1972/1973 when rebuilt and repainted. (Bailey)

COVENTRY
GRAND GALA & C
SATURDAY, JUNE 19th

Stupendous entertainment for all at the War Memorial Park

W. JOHN EVANS (Supreme International Champion Sheepdog Demonstrator)
THE ROZMARYNKA BAND (Czechoslovakia's Leading Band)
INTERNATIONAL WRESTLING (at 7 p.m.) featuring Sensational Tag Team Match
OPEN AIR STAGE featuring The Crackerjacks, Cal McCord etc.

The famous Royal Marines' Motor Cycle Display Team
KENNARDS MINIATURE CIRCUS ★ PUNCH & JUDY ★ LITTLE WALLOP
ENTERTAINING TROUPES ★ CARNIVAL AND JAZZ BANDS
ATHLETICS ★ CYCLING ★ SIX-A-SIDE FOOTBALL
Late Night entertainment by "THE MIDNIGHTS"
Pat Collins Mammoth Amusement Fair
MAGNIFICENT FIREWORKS DISPLAY

BUS SERVICES (Se
1.   STOKE HEATH - CHAPELFIELDS   16.   KERESL
                        SPECIAL BUSES BROA

TRANSPORT HEAD OFFICE,
HARNALL LANE EAST, COVENTRY
JUNE 1965

One of the many internal adverts used over many years to promote events and services in the city. In this case it is the Coventry Carnival of 1965, a very popular event that saw the city come to a standstill while it wound its way around the streets and finished up at the War Memorial Park.

CARNIVAL PROCESSION
WAR MEMORIAL PARK

Procession leaves Park at 2.15 p.m.

Gala commences at 2.45 p.m.

Admission: ADULTS 2/-   CHILDREN (under 15) 1/-

After 8.0 p.m.—ADULTS 1/-   CHILDREN (under 15) 6d.

Licensed Refreshments   Unlicensed Refreshments

g Memorial Park)

REEN LANE   17.   FENSIDE AVENUE - BROADGATE

TE - EARLSDON AVENUE

N. McDONALD, M.INST.T. GENERAL MANAGER

Also from 1965 is this advert for the Coventry Air Pageant, which amongst many things saw the flypast of the now famous Red Arrows. Back then, as a formation team, they had only just got together and this was probably one of their very first shows under that name.

PAGEANT

"ROUILLE DE FRANCE"
ACE

FALL TEAM
ay items

UNLICENSED REFRESHMENTS

ON

UST 1965

TON VILLAGE

BUS SERVICE 17A

BROADGATE
to
BAGINTON VILLAGE

AUGMENTED
AS REQUIRED

N. McDONALD. M.INST.T. GENERAL MANAGER

In 1965 the first of a number of single-deck buses arrived with fleet numbers 502–508, these being Bedford VAS with bodies by Marshall and seats for thirty people. Here is bus 502 (CRW 502C) parked up in Pool Meadow. They were sometimes used on the Berkswell service. (Bailey)

Here is bus 505 parked up in Sandy Lane garage with two of the Bedford coaches parked either side. Two of these vehicles started Coventry's first one-man operation(OMO) in 1966, linking the railway station to the city and Pool Meadow. (Bailey)

Other vehicles delivered that year were a batch of Commer minibuses, numbered 509–515. With only twelve seats they were limited in use and had been used for a number of private-hire jobs. But their main function was to carry handicapped children to school, for which some of the Bedfords were also used. This is bus 515 (CRW 515C), with the photograph taken in 1971. (Lane)

The original batch were followed by 522–531(KDU 522/523, KRW 524-531F). One of the last being bus 530, seen here parked up in Harnall Lane garage. (Bailey)

An advert from 1965, promoting the new Hillman Imp, that was released only a couple of years earlier. The reproduction here is only in black and white, but the original is in strong colours and would certainly have stood out as an advert inside a bus.

In 1966 further Daimler Fleetlines were delivered, numbered 1–22, they had East Lancs/Neepsend bodies. This is number 2 (CKV 2D), seen here at the Massey Ferguson plant in Banner Lane, being used in a competition between Leicester and Coventry to find the bus driver of the year. The competition later expanded to include other operators. Note the new style of fleet names and position of the coat of arms. (Bailey)

Bus number 6 on service 2 in its original livery. The first two (buses 1 and 2) were converted to OMO use in 1967 for trials on service 26. Four survived into ownership with WMPTE. (Bailey)

Bus number 16 in Pool Meadow, with one of the Leyland Atlanteans in the background. It would not be long before the new bus station would be built. (Travel Lens – G. Lumb)

Bus 16 also at the Massey Ferguson plant for the driver of the year competition, this time in the newer livery of Marshall red and Shetland ivory. (Bailey)

Seen in the original Broadgate, bus number 4 overtaking one of the first 8ft-wide buses delivered to the city.

An interesting comparison between different generations of buses, including bus 11 of the 1966 batch. (Greener)

The batch 516-518 Bristol RESL with ECW bodies and seats for 44 passengers, they were delivered in 1967. These were the first buses of Bristol manufacturer to be built for a municipal operator for many years. Here is bus 516 (KHP 516E) in Pool Meadow, with the Midland Red booking office behind.

Another photograph of bus 516, taken in 1967, next to one of the three Bedford coaches in Pool Meadow. These vehicles were initially used on service 19, but were later used to start service 26. (Lane)

The same bus in Pool Meadow in use on the 19 route, terminating at Eastern Green. Overtaking it is one of the Bedfords in use on the first driver-only service linking the city with the railway station.

Bus 518 painted in the later livery of Marshall red and Shetland ivory. Service 28 was started with these vehicles, but later on all six saw little further use in Coventry and were loaned for service elsewhere.(Bailey)

A good view of bus 518, showing the entrance steps. These six were the first of the RES 1 type produced. Unique bodies were carried with new type fronts but older rear curved style. (Bailey)

The other three were numbered 519–521, having forty-two-seat dual-door bodies. This is the last one, seen here parked in Pool Meadow Bus Station.

A copy of an advert promoting private-hire use of the variety of vehicles in the fleet. Issued in 1967 and produced in support of the hiring of its coach fleet.

Advert for service 26 originally started using some of the Bristol single-deckers in 1967. Later buses from the 1–22 batch were tried on the service.

The next new buses were numbered 23–40 and were Daimler Fleetlines with seventy-two-seat dual-door ECW bodies, this time designed for OMO. This is bus 25 (KWK 25F) in Pool Meadow, now with a maroon engine cover, no doubt to save constant repainting. (Bailey)

Bus 25 at Greyfriars Green in its original condition. Coventry and Manchester were the first two operators to introduce two-door one-man-operator double-deck buses into service. By the middle of 1968, they went into service as 'Monobuses', the purpose for which they were designed.

A classic shot of number 26 at the top end of the new Pool Meadow, showing that only the Sainsbury car park had been built. These buses were the first ECW double-deckers sold to a non-nationalised operator.

Bus 26, having been rebuilt and repainted in a simplified livery as part of an on-going experiment in colour schemes. It has also been rebuilt with one door along with the rest of the batch between 1973 and 1974. (Bailey)

Another bus from the batch, number 32, passing through Broadgate. (Travel Lens – G. Lumb)

Not obvious at first view, but this photograph shows Harnall Lane Depot full of buses and parked cars. One of several times when the bus crews went on strike and all the buses stayed in the depot during June 1971, the day of the carnival. (Bailey)

The front cover of the new bus timetable for the 23 route, then being converted to OMO in 1968, not long after the buses had been delivered.

Bus number 41 (KKV 41G), the first of the 41–58 batch delivered in 1969, being a Daimler Fleetline with East Lancs dual-door body and seats for seventy-two people. The photograph was taken in Sandy Lane bus garage, with other members of the fleet parked all around. (Bailey)

Bus number 47 parked up in Pool Meadow Bus Station and delivered the same year that man landed on the moon. Note the separation for passengers with cash or passes and those with tickets. (Bailey)

Bus 47 in Broadgate on the Bedworth route. A new idea was introduced that when the sidelights were turned on, the headlights came on very dimly aswell. (Bailey)

Awaiting passengers in Pool Meadow, is bus 54. Note the construction of the student accommodation for what was then the Lanchester Polytechnic. (Travel Lens – G. Lumb)

A interesting shot at the rear of Harnall Lane bus garage, showing a newly delivered bus from the 41–58 batch, next to one of the Daimler Freelines soon to be withdrawn from service. Also note the other vehicles parked up.

A photograph taken from St Michael's tower overlooking the newly built second-generation Pool Meadow Bus Station and the still-to-be completed ring road. (Bailey)

Not really part of the fleet, but certainly housed at Harnall Lane bus garage, is this Bedford which replaced the converted Daimler single-deck bus used to transport older people on trips. (Bailey).

Another view of the same vehicle, parked up near the front of the garage. (Bailey)

The first three female drivers employed by Coventry Transport. They were Maurine Bailey, Marlene Gilbert and Daphne Simms.

Bus number 63 (SWK 63J), part of the 59–76 batch of Daimler Fleetlines with Park Royal seventy-two-seat dual-door bodies, delivered in 1970. Parked up outside the entrance to Sandy Lane bus garage in the later Marshall red and Shetland ivory livery. (Bailey)

A photograph of number 64 parked up in Sandy Lane bus garage amongst other members of the current fleet. These were the first delivered in the Marshall red livery. (Bailey)

A postcard showing two of the batch in Broadgate, also with a good view of the temporary shops, which seemed to last forever.

A rare shot of bus 59, painted up in blue and cream but carrying the fleetname for Coventry Transport, ready for the transfer to the West Midlands PTE in 1974. (Bailey)

Above: A rare photograph once again, this time showing Sandy Lane bus garage closed in 1971 for the day, due to strike action. (Bailey)

Right: Another shot, taken through the railings of the line-up of buses on the day of the carnival. (Bailey)

Decimalisation D-D[ay]

Your £ s. d. Fares
WILL BE
REPLACED
by Decimal Fares

ALL CHANGE
WILL BE IN
DECIMAL COINS ONLY

If you tender £ s. d. coins please follow this chart and
TENDER HIGH
i.e. £ s. d. coins in multiples of 6d.

TRANSPORT HEAD OFFICE,
HARNALL LANE EAST,
COVENTRY

ORDINARY		
PRESENT £ s. d. FARE	NEW DECIMAL FARE	AMOUN[T] IN £
2d (PENSIONERS)	1p	6[d]
7d	3p	1/
10d	4p	1/
1/-	5p	1/
1/5d	7p	1/
1/7d	8p	2/
1/10d	9p	2/

DISCOUNT TIC[KETS]

Decimalisation came into force in 1971 and this is one of many adverts used to display the conversion value of the old coinage against the new.

TRAFFIC NOTICE

Monday 15th February 1971

	CHANGE	CHILDREN'S FARES			
		PRESENT £ s. d. FARE	NEW DECIMAL FARE	AMOUNT TO TENDER IN £ s. d. COINS	CHANGE
)	1½p				
	2p	4d	2p	6d (2½p)	½p
	1p	6d	3p	1/- (5p)	2p
	—	7d	3p	1/- (5p)	2p
)	½p	10d	4p	1/- (5p)	1p
)	2p	1/-	5p	1/- (5p)	—
)	1p	1/2d	6p	1/6 (7½p)	1½p

ARE AVAILABLE FOR ALL ADULT FARES

D. L. HYDE, C. ENG., M.I.MECH.E., A.M.Inst
GENERAL MANAGER

coventry transport

D.C.N.4.

COVENTRY CORPORATION TRANSPORT

DECIMAL CURRENCY NOTES

ALWAYS THINK DECIMAL CURRENCY

This slogan cannot be stressed too much.

If you are thinking right you will not make the mistake of thinking and counting:—

6d as 6 new pence instead of 2½ new pence
1/- as 12 new pence instead of 5 new pence
1/6d as 18 new pence instead of 7½ new pence
2/- as 24 new pence instead of 10 new pence
Particularly the first and third ones.

Think of your fares in decimal — start now

ADULT FARES				CHILDRENS FARES			
Present £. s. d. Fares	Decimal Fares	Amount to be Tendered	Change	Present £. s. d. Fares	Decimal Fares	Amount to be Tendered	Change
7d	3p	1/- (5p)	2p	4d	2p	6d (2½p)	½p
10d	4p	1/- (5p)	1p	6d	3p	1/- (5p)	2p
1/-	5p	1/- (5p)	—	7d	3p	1/- (5p)	2p
1/5d	7p	1/6d (7½p)	½p	10d	4p	1/- (5p)	1p
1/7d	8p	2/- (10p)	2p	1/-	5p	1/- (5p)	—
1/10d	9p	2/- (10p)	1p	1/2d	6p	1/6d (7½p)	1½p

Another advert, this time on a leaflet, helping people to better understand the conversion rates.

The next batch of buses to arrive did so in 1971, being numbered 77–94, and were again Daimler Fleetlines with East Lancs seventy-two-seat dual-door bodies. This is number 85 (YHP 485J) in Pool Meadow showing the De Vere Hotel being built in the background. (Bailey)

Last of the batch, number 94, in Pool Meadow. Six of the batch were loaned to Oxford in 1973 to help with a bus shortage. All were later converted to a single-door layout. (Bailey)

In 1972 Daimler Fleetlines with East Lancs bodywork for seventy-four passengers arrived. Numbered 95–122, these were the first buses for some time with only one door and not two. This is number 96 (YVC 96K) in the bus station. (Bailey)

Bus 103, decked out in posters to promote the store Owen Owen, running a special service from various parts of the city to the shop in Broadgate. (Bailey)

A replacement coach for the three Bedfords was number 407 (YVC 407L), a Ford R226, forty-nine-seat Plaxton delivered in 1972 and seen here at the front of Harnall Lane garage. (Bailey)

Another delivery in 1972 was bus 408 (GWK 408L), a Ford Transit, seen here after transfer to the West Midlands PTE in 1975. (Lane)

Buses 123–142 (A mixture of GWK L, PDU M registrations), Daimler Fleetlines with seventy-four-seat East Lancs bodies, were the last buses delivered for service in the city in 1973. This is bus 137 in Pool Meadow.

Ordered, but actually delivered after ownership had changed to West Midlands PTE, were what became 4447–4466. This is 4450 (ROK 450M) in Harnall Lane bus garage with West Midlands fleet names. (Bailey)

FOUR
DEMONSTRATORS AND COVENTRY BUSES AFTER SERVICE

Over the years, many buses have been 'sent to Coventry' to be demonstrated, the manufacturer hoping it would result in orders for new vehicles. In reality this rarely happened, but these outsiders often added variety to the local bus scene. The following is a small selection. Here is the revolutionary AEC Q (AMV 433), in service in Coventry for well over a year in the 1930s. Unlike conventional vehicles at the time, which had the engine at the front, this had a side engine and came with a very modern-looking body style. (Travel Lens)

This is the famous Daimler Fleetline demonstrator (HP 7000), painted in Birmingham Corporation colours, but which saw service all over the country. Here it is seen in service on route 22 in Coventry.

Left: Another shot of this pioneer bus, this time in Pool Meadow Bus Station, with a young boy transfixed by it when he probably should be off to school! This bus was later destroyed in the disastrous fire at Blue Bus of Willington Depot.

Below: A Leyland Panther with Roe bodywork (CRH 175C) due for service in Kingston-upon-Hull, but here demonstrating its capabilities for possible OMO in 1965.

A Bristol RE (HWU 641C), also tested out for possible use in 1966, with stickers saying 'On Hire to Coventry Transport Dept.' in the side window. Later, a small batch of similar vehicles entered service in the city.

An interesting vehicle tried in Coventry was the SELNEC prototype EX1, which was used on the 16 route and is seen here at the Shepherd and Shepherdess terminus. (Bailey)

Every bus fleet has service vehicles to help keep things running smoothly. Such vehicles would include a breakdown tender, which in this case is a AEC Matador (PO 3922) that served the city for many years after being bought in 1939.

A replacement breakdown vehicle came in the guise of a Bedford RL (PGW 476). (Travel Lens – G. Lumb)

Ever wondered where old Coventry buses went? Well, in the case of bus 213, it went on holiday to Europe as a Sundecker! One can only wonder what the holidaymakers would have said if they had known about the origins of this vehicle!

SUNDECKER

Join our travelling grandstand — unlimited sunbathing and all-round sightseeing.

Come on your own, or with friends and meet other young Europeans. Travel the backroads through France, Spain or Morocco, through Greece, Scandinavia or Italy.

We don't travel fast, but we suntan faster. To keep the cost down we camp at night, SUNDECKER provides all the equipment.

Each traveller has 2 seats — one on the lower deck — reclining aircraft type — and one on top, and by joining Suntrekkers in Europe, all your holiday is spent travelling leisurely, and not in a rush from the Channel ports.

Here are a few of our tours —

MOROCCO £199 ex Malaga 14 days

DATES:

Depart - Return	Depart - Return	Depart - Return
05.04 - 18.04	07.06 - 20.06	02.08 - 15.08
19.04 - 02.05	21.06 - 04.07	23.08 - 05.09
10.05 - 23.05	05.07 - 18.07	06.09 - 19.09
24.05 - 06.06	19.07 - 01.08	20.09 - 03.10
		04.10 - 17.10

FRANCE £175 ex Basle 13 days

DATES:

Depart - Return	Depart - Return	Depart - Return
27.06 - 09.07	01.08 - 13.08	05.09 - 17.09
06.07 - 16.07	08.08 - 20.08	19.09 - 01.10
11.07 - 23.07	15.08 - 27.08	03.10 - 16.10
18.07 - 06.08	22.08 - 03.09	

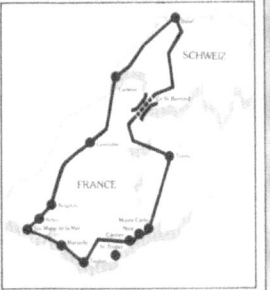

ITALY £113 ex Zurich 7 days

DATES:

Depart - Return	Depart - Return	Depart - Return
28.06 - 04.07	26.07 - 01.08	23.08 - 29.08
05.07 - 11.07	02.08 - 08.08	30.08 - 05.09
12.07 - 18.07	09.08 - 15.08	06.09 - 12.09
19.07 - 25.07	16.08 - 22.08	

SUNDECKER also run other itineraries of 4-43 days (full details are in our brochure).

Tours depart from Basle, Zurich or Malaga. Transport to these departure points is **not** included in the tour cost, but can be arranged by us.

SAMPLE COSTS RETURN:	Rail	Rail, up to age 26	Air	Bus
ZURICH	82	51	74	66
MALAGA	—	79	72	88
BASLE	—	63	78	65

For full details see the Sundecker brochure — phone us for your copy, or ask to see your travel agent's office copy.

SUNDECKER — OPEN TOP EUROPE Tours operated by SSR Reisen, Zurich.
General Sales Agents in the U.K.
TREKAMERICA 62 Kenway Road London SW5. 01-373 5085

The rear of the poster, listing the places to be visited and how much it would cost to travel on an old Coventry Transport bus!

One of a number of buses now in preservation, This is bus 94, a Daimler CVA6, seen here in the old Keresley Works, Watery Lane, only weeks before the whole complex was pulled down. Therefore, this was the last bus to visit and leave the famous works. (Bailey)

The same bus but this time passing the old Pool Meadow Midland Red enquiry office and cafe, which was about to be knocked down, as can be seen by the boarded-up windows in the building behind. (Bailey)

A special trip was organised to travel around bus 94, taking in some of the routes that would have once been served by such buses. Here it is seen in company with the new number 94, and twenty years separated both designs. (Bailey)

Two old Coventry buses now looked after by the Coventry Transport Museum. Bus 366, a wartime delivery but re-bodied post-war by Roe, was withdrawn in 1959 and converted into a mobile workshop, later being presented for preservation in 1971 to the local museum. (Bailey)

Another bus in the Coventry Transport Museum is this Daimler Fleetline, the last to be built at the Radford works. It was donated for preservation and converted into an open top. As can be seen by the livery, it was the bus they transported the football team around the city with after they won the FA Cup in 1987. (Bailey)

A bus that survived being broken up and is currently owned by Derby Museums, is the single-deck bus 244, a 1940 Daimler. It was sold to Derby for further service in late 1949.

Three Coventry buses lined up in the War Memorial Park, ready to run in formation to the new Pool Meadow Bus Station as part of its official opening. (Bailey)

Lord Mayor Councillor Nick Nolan in the process of opening the new bus station, he is flanked by ex-crew Maurine and Jim Bailey. (Bailey)

After so many years, its amazing that anything still survives relating to the Coventry Tramway system. These tram tracks are still visible today, as part of the old Foleshill Depot where much of the tramline is still in the ground. (Bailey)

This shot of the tramlines at the back of Harnall Lane bus garage, known as Priestley's Bridge, was taken a few years ago. (Bailey)

Even more incredibly, at least three trams survived into the last part of the twentieth century. Tram 32, stored in a place called Maxstoke, not far from Coventry, just rotted away, but was still recognisable in the early 1990s, as the photographs show. This is an outside shot of tram 32. (Bailey)

The interior shot showing its fleet number, which along with other information was still very much visible. (Bailey)

The big surprise was tram 71, which found its way to Guildford – maybe via canal? It has now gone into preservation. Here is an external shot. (Bailey)

The interior photograph shows its fleet number, tram 71, plus its seating capacity and Brush works transfer. (Bailey)

Tram 68 survived just off Butts Lane until 2000. Whatever could be salvaged was, including the end bulkheads. What is left is seen here as part of a greenhouse. (Bailey)

To finish off this section, here is a photograph of a new-style bus shelter tried out at the bus stop outside Coventry Theatre.

FIVE
OTHER OPERATORS

PARLOR COACHES, Ltd.

Phone:
City 8028-9

Reg. Office:
9-10 PANCRAS LANE,
E.C.4.

Regular Services.

Coaches Leave

LONDON

(EMBANKMENT—Charing Cross Station Underground)

TWICE DAILY. SUNDAYS INCLUDED.

At **9** a.m. and **6.30** p.m.

For

COVENTRY

Calling en route **DUNSTABLE FENNY STRATFORD, STONY STRATFORD, TOWCESTER, WEEDON, DAVENTRY** and **DUNCHURCH.**

Also for

Warwick & Leamington

Leave London **9** a.m.

Coaches leave **LONDON** (Embankment, Charing Cross Station Underground) Daily **6.30** p.m. for

BUCKINGHAM

For **Fares** see over.

Other companies have brought people to visit the city for many years, but it has not always been obvious to say the least. This is an old poster, recently discovered, which offered a daily service between London and Coventry. One can only assume there must have been a demand for such a link.

	FARES.		Single	Day Return	Period Return
					availabl 2 months
LONDON and	LEAMINGTON and WARWICK	...	9/6	12/6	14/0
,,	,, COVENTRY	...	9/0	10/6	14/0
,,	,, DAVENTRY	...	7/0	—	10/6
,,	,, WEEDON	...	6/9	—	10/0
,,	,, TOWCESTER	...	5/6	—	8/6
,,	,, BUCKINGHAM	...	6/-	8/-	9/6
,,	,, STONY STRATFORD		5/0	7/0	8/6
,,	,, FENNY STRATFORD		4/6	6/0	8/0
,,	,, DUNSTABLE	...	3/-	4/-	5/6

All Seats must be Booked in Advance.

Date of Return must be stated at time of Booking for Period Returns,

Tickets may be obtained from the following Agents:

Phone

WARWICK.—Mr. A. R. DODD, 9 Jury Street.   Warwick 159
LEAMINGTON.—W. H. SMITH & SONS, Booksellers, Parade.
COVENTRY.—E. V. DODMAN, Ltd., Far Gosford Street. C'try 2268
   E. P. SADLER, Paynes Lane.
   ROSE'S GARAGE, 210 Bell Green Road.   Coventry 8118
   J. TYLER, Tobacconist, opposite Broadway Cinema, Albany
      Road, Earlsdon.
   BANTAM COACHES, Walsgrave Road, Stoke.
   J. JAMES, Post Office, Exhall.
   J. W. KENT, 42 Hertford Street.
   S. T. SIBLEY, Tile Hill Lane Garage.   Coventry 4503
DUNCHURCH.—Mr. FAULKNER, Confectioner & Tobacconist.
DAVENTRY.—WHEATSHEAF HOTEL.   Daventry 16
WEEDON.—W. H. CORBY, Tobacconist, 34 High Street.
TOWCESTER.—DARBY'S GARAGE.
STONY STRATFORD.—THE BULL HOTEL. (Mr. Pugh).
FENNY STRATFORD.—THE BULL HOTEL. (Mr. Owen).
DUNSTABLE.—BLAKE'S GARAGE, High Street.
LONDON AGENTS.—
ADAMS & Co., 7 High Street, Wood Green.   Mountview 6768
The CENTRAL LONDON STATION, Crescent Place
   Cartwright Gardens, W.C.1.
EMPIRE BOOKING OFFICE, 210 Church Street,
   Notting Hill Gate.   Park 9393
GREYHOUND MOTORS. Ltd., 229 Hammersmith
   Road, W.6.   Riverside 4273
W. GREEVES, 7-10 Church Street, Camberwell, S.E.   Rodney 2841
IDEAL TEA ROOMS, (A. C. Pocock), 17 High Street,
   North Finchley.   Finchley 3141
NELSON TOURS, Ltd., 8 Grand Hotel Buildings,
   Trafalgar Square.   Gerrard 8343
STOCKWELL SERVICE STATION, 189 Clapham
   Road, S.W.9.   Brixton 1951
WEEDEN & SON, General Ironmongers, 82 Junction Road, Upper
   Holloway.   Mountview, 7401
And **THOMAS TRANSPORT, Ltd.,** 12 Villiers
   Street, Charing Cross.   Gerrard 4526-7

The other side of the same poster indicates prices and where tickets can be bought from. The list of agents is of great interest, especially those associated with Coventry.

COVENTRY

LONDON

NON-STOP DAILY
MOTORWAY EXPRESS

FARES

15/- SINGLE   **23/3** DAY RETURN   **24/6** PERIOD RETURN

SATURDAYS
(Whit Saturday to end of September inclusive)

16/9 SINGLE   **25/9** DAY RETURN   **27/-** PERIOD RETURN

SCHEDULE

		a.m.	p.m.	p.m.
LONDON (Victoria Coach Station)	depart	9.30	12.30	7.00
COVENTRY (Pool Meadow)	arrive	12.00	3.00	9.30
COVENTRY (Pool Meadow)	depart	a.m. 8.30	p.m. 1.00	p.m. 7.00
LONDON (Victoria Coach Station)	arrive	11.00	3.30	9.30

YOUR TICKET GUARANTEES YOU A SEAT

BOOKING MADE

Tickets may be obtained from

LONDON COASTAL C
VICTORIA COACH STATIO
BUCKINGHAM PALACE R

Telephone: SLOane 0202

and at

ALL AGENTS

TRAVEL AGENTS

PRINTED IN ENGLAND BY GREEN & WELBURN LIMIT

Of even greater interest is this leaflet, used to promote a day visit to Coventry for people who lived in London. It dates back to 1961. It was operated by Midland Red, clearly using their fleet of motorway coaches, and probably was a way to fill seats when the coaches were on a return journey.

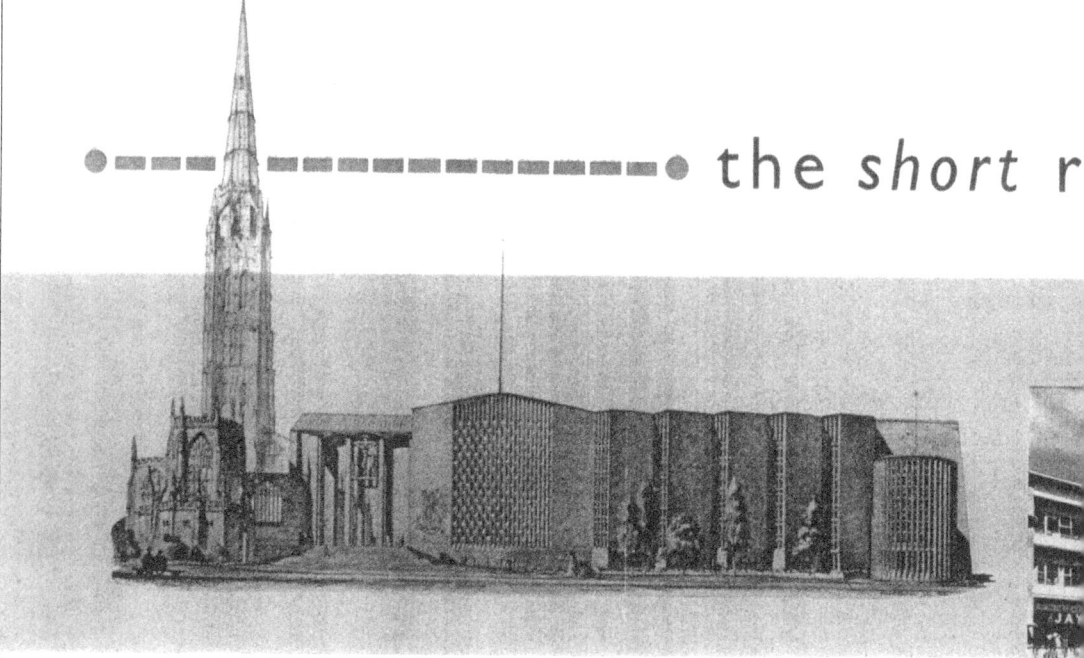

the *short r*

The new Coventry Cathedral

▶ **the simplest, easiest way to travel**

te to Coventry

The Precinct

en hours in a wonderful city

ery old. In spite of the war-time havoc it
with its ancient buildings which proclaim its
St. Mary's Hall is regarded as one of the
guild halls in the country.

remarkable new Cathedral, now nearing
n architectural interest and splendour it will
mpel a visit.

e Precinct shopping centre, so modern in its
t it sets a pattern for the world of the future.

heatre—a civic venture—has already achieved
rthy of a visit.

tatue of Lady Godiva perpetuates the link
e and distant years.

The inside of the leaflet was even more interesting and was issued after part of the city had already been rebuilt. It is interesting that back in the 1960s people realised the city was very old and not the modern place visitors today think.

One of the main operators into Coventry, as seen on the previous pages, was of course Midland Red. Here is a D7, entering service in the middle of the 1950s. Number 4514, worked the route to Leicester and waits in the Midland Red section of Pool Meadow. (Bailey)

Seen in Coventry, probably on a learner duty, is a single-deck S10, number 3635, and entered service in 1950, being withdrawn from passenger service in 1964. (Bailey)

Bus number 4019, an LD8 based on the Leyland Titan, entering service in 1952. It is seen here passing through Meriden on the famous 159 route, later renumbered the 900 by West Midlands PTE after it had taken over.

A motorway coach waiting to depart for London with the fleet number 5295. It was a lucky catch on film as it was the CM6T prototype. It entered service in 1963 and is seen here in Coventry during 1967. (Lane)

Here is Leyland Leopard, number 5779, getting ready for its run to London. (Bailey)

A Daimler Fleetline, number 6182, waiting in Coventry for passengers before it made its way to Warwick. (Bailey)

Motorway Express

(Bus Station) **NUNEATON**
(Market Place) **BEDWORTH**
(Pool Meadow) **COVENTRY**

and

(Victoria Coach Station) **LONDON**

DAILY SERVICE, NON-STOP

In operation 16th April 1962

'*The Friendly Midland Red*'

Front cover of the Midland Red leaflet promoting the service that linked Coventry to London via the M1.

A Daimler Fleetline, numbered 6095, after conversion to open-top configuration. It is seen here on its run from Coventry to Warwick via Royal Leamington Spa, passing Coventry Cathedral. (Bailey)

Other operators who came into Coventry included Hall Brothers, running a regular service from the Tyne & Wear area bringing people to Coventry, sometimes to work in the factories and in the coal mines. The company was later taken over by Barton.

TAB 1710/2 TAB 1710/1
BB 188/38   BB 188/39

SOUTH SHIELDS — COVENTRY

INLAND ROUTE: Express Service **X81**
COAST ROUTE: Express Service **X82**

DAY SERVICES: DAILY THROUGHOUT THE YEAR EXCEPT CHRISTMAS DAY.
NIGHT SERVICES: FRIDAY AND SUNDAY NIGHTS THROUGHOUT THE YEAR EXCEPT CHRISTMAS NIGHT, SATURDAY NIGHTS FROM WHIT SATURDAY TO THE THIRD SATURDAY IN SEPTEMBER INCLUSIVE, ALSO CHRISTMAS EVE AND THE NIGHT OF BOXING DAY.

X82 Read down	X81 Read down	X82 Read down	X81 Read down		X81 Read up	X82 Read up	X81 Read up	X82 Read up
0830	0845	2030	2045	SOUTH SHIELDS (Bath Street)	0645	0710	1845	1910
0842	......	2042	......	Whitburn (East Street)	......	0700	......	1900
0900	......	2100	......	Sunderland (Stockton Road)	......	0650	......	1850
0913	......	2113	......	New Seaham (Deneside) Bus Stop	......	0635	......	1835
0923	......	2123	......	Easington (Brown's Shop)	......	0625	......	1825
......	0930	......	2130	NEWCASTLE (Marlborough Crescent)	0615	......	1815	......
0930	......	2130	......	Horden (Central Bus Stop)	......	0620	......	1820
0935	......	2135	......	Blackhall (Hardwick Hotel)	......	0615	......	1815
0950	......	2150	......	West Hartlepool (United Bus Station)	......	0600	......	1800
0955	......	2155	......	Seaton Carew (Bus Station)	......	0555	......	1755
......	1000	......	2200	Chester-le-Street (North Burns)	0555	......	1755	......
1010	......	2210	......	Haverton Hill (Wellington Hotel)	......	0540	......	1740
1015	......	2215	......	Billingham (Billingham Arms, Town Centre)	......	0535	......	1735
......	1020	......	2220	DURHAM (Waddington Street)	0535	......	1735	......
1030	......	2230	......	Stockton (High Street, Platform 1)	......	0525	......	1725
......	......	......	......	Ferryhill (Bus Stand)	......	......	......	......
......	1035	......	2235	Ferryhill (Bus Stand)	0520	......	1720	......
1105	1105	2305	2305	Darlington (United Bus Station)	0455	0455	1655	1655
1130	1130	2330	2330	Catterick (County Hotel)	0430	0430	1630	1630
1145	1145	2345	2345	Leeming (Motel)	0420	0420	1620	1620
1200	1200	2400	2400	Leeming (Motel)	0405	0405	1605	1605
1225	1225	0025	0025	Boroughbridge (Post Office)	0340	0340	1540	1540
1245	1245	0045	0045	Wetherby (Market Place)	0315	0315	1515	1515
1345	1345	0145	0145	Doncaster (Waterdale)	0215	0215	1415	1415
1425	1425	0225	0225	Doncaster (Waterdale)	0135	0135	1335	1335
1448	1448	0248	0248	Langold (Doncaster Road)	0110	0110	1310	1310
1500	1500	0300	0300	Worksop (Victoria Square)	0058	0058	1258	1258
1517	1517	0317	0317	Warsop (Chemist's Shop, Church Street)	0040	0040	1240	1240
1530	1530	0330	0330	Mansfield (Leeming Street)	0030	0030	1230	1230
1600	1600	0400	0400	Nottingham (Victoria Bus Station)	2355	2355	1155	1155
1615	1615	0415	0415	Nottingham (Victoria Bus Station)	2340	2340	1140	1140
1620	1620	0420	0420	Nottingham (Broad Marsh Bus Station)	2335	2335	1135	1135
1645	1645	0445	0445	Loughborough (Bus Station)	2305	2305	1105	1105
1720	1720	0520	0520	Leicester (St. Margaret's Bus Station)	2235	2235	1035	1035
1755	1755	0555	0555	Hinckley (Bus Station)	2200	2200	1000	1000
1805	1805	0605	0605	Nuneaton (Harefield Bus Station)	2150	2150	0950	0950
1815	1815	0615	0615	Bedworth (Paynes Garage, Leicester Road)	2140	2140	0940	0940
1830	1830	0630	0630	COVENTRY (Pool Meadow)	2120	2120	0920	0920

Operated subject to the General Regulations and Conditions of the Company.

All correspondence and tickets relating to services X81 and X82 should be addressed to Barton Transport Limited, 6 Cornwallis Street, South Shields (Phone: South Shields 3621).

LEICESTER (155 Uppingham Road) – SOUTHSEA (Coach Park, Clarence Esplanade) Express Service **X74**

Period of Operation: Friday, 19th May, Saturday, 20th May and Sunday, 21st May, then every Saturday until 23rd September, 1972.

	S	S	F	Su		S	S	Su	Su
LEICESTER (St. Margaret's Bus Station)	0812	1742	1742	0812	SOUTHSEA (Clarence Pier Coach Park)	1200	1500	1500	1700
Lutterworth (Greyhound)	0826	1756	1756	0826	Portsmouth (The Hard)	1204	1504	1504	1704
Rugby (Dunchurch Road, Warwick Street End)	0838	1808	1808	0838	Southampton (The Cenotaph)	1238	1538	1538	1738
Winchester (King Alfred's Statue)	1220	2150	2150	1220	Winchester (King Alfred's Statue)	1302	1602	1602	1802
Southampton (The Cenotaph)	1248	2218	2218	1248	Rugby (Dunchurch Road, Warwick Street End)	1640	1940	1940	2140
Portsmouth (The Hard)	1318	2248	2248	1318	Lutterworth (Greyhound)	1655	1955	1955	2155
SOUTHSEA (Clarence Pier Coach Park)	1322	2252	2252	1322	LEICESTER (St. Margaret's Bus Station)	1715	2015	2015	2215

	Adult	Child
Period Return	2·85	1·90
Fare Table: – Day Return	2·10	1·40
Single	1·55	1·30

Su — Sundays Only
F — Fridays Only
S — Saturdays Only
■ — July and August Only

180472 Y/TL-10000

EXPRESS SERVICE **X81** — SOUTH SHIELDS, NEWCASTLE-UPON-TYNE, DURHAM, DONCASTER, NOTTINGHAM, LEICESTER, COVENTRY

EXPRESS SERVICE **X82** — SOUTH SHIELDS, SUNDERLAND, HARTLEPOOL, DONCASTER, NOTTINGHAM, LEICESTER, COVENTRY

BARTON TRANSPORT LIMITED

HEAD OFFICE: CHILWELL, HALL BROS. (SOUTH SHIELDS) LTD, ROBIN HOOD (COACHES) LTD, HUNTINGDON ST, NOTTINGHAM
Telephone: NOTTINGHAM 55717 / NOTTINGHAM 15480
South Shields Office: 6 CORNWALLIS ST, Telephone: SOUTH SHIELDS 3621
Newcastle-upon-Tyne Office: MARLBOROUGH CRESCENT, Telephone: NEWCASTLE 22200

APRIL 1972

ALL PREVIOUS ISSUES CANCELLED

Timetable as operated under Barton ownership.

The original Hall Brothers route, as promoted on a poster.

Other companies included Standerwick, using their famous double-deck coaches entitled 'Gay Hostesses'. Here is one in Coventry. (Bailey)

A number of the Standerwick coaches parked up in Coventry loading up passengers. They started entering service in 1959 and eventually totalled a fleet-size of thirty-seven between Ribble, Standerwick and Scout – all associated with each other. (Greener)

For many years during the Coventry holiday fortnight, when the factories closed down, many people would go away on holiday. With low car ownership, people would travel by coach to their destinations. This led to a large amount of coaches leaving at the same time on the same day as soon as the holiday fortnight started. Fifty years ago, buses would run along many city routes starting from 4.45 a.m., feeding people into Pool Meadow. This photograph only partly captures the moment, taken a few years ago, with mostly Harry Shaw coaches waiting for their passengers. (Bailey)

Left: Space is limited, but over the next five pages, is coverage of some of the coach operators based in the city. This is a wonderful series of adverts as seen in an issue of the *Coventry Evening Telegraph* of 1954.

Opposite; This is a leaflet from the Red House Motor Services based in Cromwell Street, who eventually bought out the majority of other coach companies in the city by the late 1960s. These were Bunty, BTS and Godiva Bantam. Back then, previous to this, such names as Highfield (Chambers-Highfield Garage); Grove Coaches (Alfall Road) later Bonas (Supremes); Elliott Bros (Cross Road); R. Bolton (Coventry Street); Binley Motors (Heritage-Brandon Road later Cox Street); Whitley Motors (Davies-Ashington Grove) and even A.C. Wickman's. who provided works transport were in existence, to name but a few.

Travel as the Team travels,
by

Red House Motor Services
Cromwell Street, Coventry
TELEPHONE: 89004

26, 30, 33, 35, 37, 39, 41 Seaters for Hire

Private Parties OUR Speciality

DAILY TRIPS TO ALL PARTS

R.H.M.S.		R.H.M.S.
Booking Office		Booking Office
Pool Meadow		Pool Meadow
Phone: 89006		Phone: 89006

Always at Your Service

An advert by the company Reading who built the fourteen-seat body on this Karrier destined for use by RHMS. This is one of five such vehicles delivered between 1952 and 1953. All had been withdrawn by the end of the 1950s.

A classic photograph of an AEC Regal IV with Burlingham Seagull body delivered in 1951 to BTS, as part of a batch of five (KVC 894–898). The location is outside their garage in Broad Street while the business was bought by RHMS in 1967. (Bailey Collection)

Bunty was a good-size business who sold out to RHMS in 1962. This is a Maudslay Marathon III with Burlingham body for thirty-three passengers, delivered in 1950 before being sold in 1962.

Coach company Godiva, based in Ford Street, choose local manufacturer Maudslay when purchasing new vehicles. This example, KWK614, was a Marathon III with Gurney Nutting body for thirty-seven passengers. It was withdrawn in 1962. (Bailey Collection)

The companies Godiva and Bantam became one when they were incorporated under the Companies Act on 21 August 1959, but the licences of Bantam had already been acquired in 1957. Bantam had been based on the Walsgrave Road, while the combined operation was based for a time in Humber Road. This was a Ford Thames with Duple body, one of two delivered in 1961. The company became part of the RHMS group in the late 1960s.